MODERN
flower arranging

STEP-BY-STEP INSTRUCTIONS FOR MODERN DESIGNS

TERESA P. LANKER

TALMAGE MCLAURIN

INTRODUCTION

FLORAL DESIGN is constantly evolving. Trends in color, fashion and decorating, as well as shifts in lifestyles, hobbies and interests, influence the looks and styles that are popular with designers and with consumers. Though some arrangements never go out of style, shifts in trends influence the way these standards are composed, accessorized or stylized. While familiar arrangements are routinely reimagined, new design ideas evolve to establish the trends of the modern era.

This book is intended for floral designers who seek to advance beyond traditional everyday arranging. It offers step-by-step instructions for designs that run the gamut from updated classics to current and emerging trends. Twenty fresh design concepts are offered, each with three design variations. The design process for each arrangement is described in four detailed steps along with the fresh flower recipe. While specific flower types are identified, endless variations can be achieved by adjusting the flower types and colors. Some styles are suitable for special events, others for everyday orders with a twist or for customers who want something different. Though the principles of floral design are not specifically addressed, a knowledge of good design is assumed and should guide design decisions including the choice and use of design elements.

Readers are encouraged to use this book for education and inspiration. By experimenting with these modern design concepts, designers will advance to new creative levels of floral skill and artistry, and may ultimately springboard to setting new trends in modern flower arranging.

TABLE OF CONTENTS

OMBRÉ

Ombré is a modern twist on the monochromatic color harmony that emphasizes a progression of one hue from light to dark or dark to light. Here, three designs are presented with varying approaches to the rhythmic transition, including top to bottom, side to side and circling around a wreath form.

FRESH MATERIALS:

Allium

Rose

Carnation

Lisianthus

Trachelium

Philodendron

Miniature calla

This red-violet composition utilizes limited foliage in order to keep the emphasis on color transition versus contrast.

Position seven stems of *Allium* at a height about 2½ times the height of the container so the stems radiate in a "V" shape. Allow each flower its own space.

Add eight or nine roses, creating a comparable level beneath the *Allium*. Add 10 to 12 carnations beneath the roses, allowing a few to intermix.

Add a few lisianthuses and *Trachelium* deep beneath the carnations Then extend the sides with additional lisianthuses and expand the frothy base with more *Trachelium*.

Add a few *Philodendron* leaves to the background within the lower portion of the design. Then add a few miniature callas to the midsection to add style and enhance the color blend.

Ombré

This modern centerpiece based in the red hue offers a
strong transition from rich burgundy shades on the left
to the palest tints of pink cream on the right, creating a
natural visual rhythm.

FRESH MATERIALS:

Dahlia
Galax leaf
Cymbidium orchid
Rosa 'Milano'
Lilium 'Sorbonne'
Parrot tulip
Astilbe

Wrap a decorative ribbon around a horizontal container and secure it in back with hot glue or glue dots. Beginning on the left end of the container, position a group of *Dahlias* close to the foam. Add *Galax* leaves beneath the *Dahlias* and layer *Cymbidium* orchids in water picks over the *Dahlias*.

Directly beside the *Dahlia* group, create a cluster of roses with an equivalent height and width. Vary the roses' depths to provide a sense of dimension. Add *Galax* leaves beneath.

Add two or three lilies next to the roses, with the open flowers facing slightly to the right.

Finish the right end of the container with a group of parrot tulips that follow the directional flow of the lilies. Supplement the tulip group with lily buds and *Astilbe* until this group is similar in size and volume to the rest of the design.

Ombré

Patterned groupings of green flowers with a touch of
foliage and a Flexi grass shelter provide a fresh approach
to the traditional round centerpiece.

FRESH MATERIALS:

Hydrangea

Dianthus 'Green Trick'

Anthurium

Salal

Flexi grass

1

Position a floral foam design ring atop a decorative riser. Use three stems of *Hydrangea* to create a cluster close to the foam. Repeat this step two more times, making sure the three resulting groups are spaced equidistant from one another.

2

To the right of each group of *Hydrangea*, create a similar low cluster using five stems of *Dianthus* 'Green Trick'. Make sure the stems are positioned to provide coverage from the inside edge to the outside edge.

3

Group three *Anthurium* into each of the remaining spaces around the ring. Position the spadix of each flower in nearly the same direction to create a sense of circular flow.

4

Add a few salal leaves as needed to fill in areas of exposed foam. Loop stems of Flexi grass over the top of the wreath, inserting the tip and stem ends into varying locations around the ring until the desired intersecting shelter is formed. Add a butterfly accent to one of the *Dianthus* clusters, if desired.

CUBED

Flower arrangements designed in cube-shaped containers have a strong sense of geometry that looks fresh and modern. Whether the flowers follow a boxy outline or are given the freedom to ramble past the edges, cube designs offer the opportunity to juxtapose the curved lines of natural materials against the straight lines of the vessel.

FRESH MATERIALS:
Hydrangea (miniature)
Gerbera
Rose
Spray rose
Button mum
Nigella
Veronica
Black lichen
Flexi grass

This tussie-mussie-style design features a collection of petite blossoms beneath a Flexi grass shelter that cleverly repeats the cube shape of the container.

1

Fill the cube with floral foam level with the container edge. Insert flowers into a low, dense mass. Place the *Hydrangea*, *Gerbera* and roses first, followed by spray roses and button mums to fill gaps at the edges. Then, add the *Nigella* and *Veronica*, allowing slightly longer stems to extend beyond the mass. Tuck in black lichen where needed to cover the foam.

2

Make two sharp bends in a stem of Flexi grass, creating a line about equivalent to the width of the container and stem ends that form two perpendicular angles. Insert the ends of the Flexi grass into the back of the container until the crossbar above the flowers is about equal to the height of the container.

3

Repeat Step 2 with three additional stems of Flexi grass, spacing them one in front of the other until reaching the front edge of the container.

4

Add a pair of intersecting Flexi grass stems placed off-center in the opposite direction. Allow these stems slightly more height than the first four to enhance the depth and dimension of the finished design.

Cubed

Bleached, stripped willow sticks extend a wooden box to
create one cube atop another with a simple floral cap.

FRESH MATERIALS:
Salal
Carnation
Anthurium
Eryngium
Spray rose

1

Place a liner slightly smaller than the wooden cube inside the container and fill edge to edge with floral foam that stands twice the height of the container. Add bleached, stripped willow sticks between the two containers at a height just above the foam.

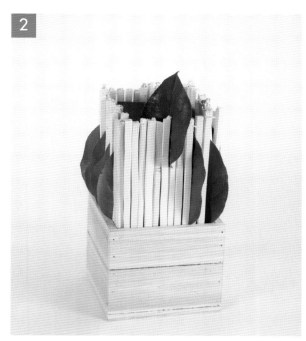

2

Slide an individual salal leaf between two sticks so only one edge is visible. Repeat for a total of four or five leaves per side, spacing the leaves evenly.

3

Cut the stems of four carnations to about 1½ inches, and insert them into the top of the foam block, creating a square.

4

Add a pair of *Anthuriums* in a low, stacked profile over the center of the carnations. Accent the top with *Eryngium* and spray roses.

Cubed

*Autumn-inspired flowers, grouped into bundles and
loosely arranged in this ribbon-wrapped container,
create an easy, casual centerpiece.*

FRESH MATERIALS:

Leucadendron

Rosa 'Milva'

Hypericum

Dahlia

Alstroemeria

Hydrangea

Pincushion protea

Kangaroo paw

Ninebark

1

Cut a piece of patterned burlap ribbon long enough to wrap around the exterior of the cube. Use adhesive dots to adhere one edge of the ribbon to the container. Wrap around and then secure the ribbon to itself with additional adhesive dots. Add about an inch of pea gravel to the container, and fill with properly prepared flower food solution.

2

Group flowers by type (*Leucadendron*, rose, *Hypericum*, *Dahlia*, *Alstroemeria*), and bundle them into small handfuls. Bind each bundle with wire or raffia, and cut stems so each bundle is slightly longer than the height of the cube. Place one flower bundle in each corner, with stems in the gravel for security, making sure to vary the flower colors and forms.

3

Add a bundle of *Alstroemeria* to the center followed by a single *Hydrangea* to the left and a single pincushion protea to the right.

4

Create a bundle of kangaroo paws with stems a few inches longer than the others. Add this bundle off-center to create an asymmetrical accent. Use individual stems of ninebark as needed to fill gaps and provide contrast between groups.

GROWING

This collection of whimsical designs incorporates the look of plants and flowers as they are grown in containers and in gardens. Each highlights the way flowers are found in nature while allowing artistic freedom and interpretation.

FRESH MATERIALS:
Carnation
Honeysuckle

A carnation-covered sphere provides an unexpected backdrop for a naturally rambling honeysuckle vine. The aged container provides an old-world sensibility that perfectly complements the modern mix.

1

Soak a 4-inch floral-foam sphere. Fluff open the blossoms of 50 carnations, and cut the stems to about 1 inch past the base of the calyx.

2

Insert the carnations side-by-side into the foam sphere until it is fully covered and evenly shaped.

3

Place the flower-covered sphere in a decorative urn so that at least ⅔ of the sphere sits above the lip of the container.

4

Insert honeysuckle vines into the upper portion of the sphere in an asymmetrical manner. Use long, light-gauge florist wire bent into hairpins to hold the cascading vines into position.

Growing

This authentic presentation of roses in a modern vintage style is given added appeal by the cloche enclosure, the ivy that "grows" through it and the mossy base complete with scattered petals.

FRESH MATERIALS:

Rosa 'Mariatheresia'
Sweet William
Eucalyptus
Ivy

Paint a terra-cotta pot and saucer with alternating bursts of dark green, medium green and white paints, and smudge the wet paint with a damp sponge to achieve an aged finish. Add a plastic or foil liner and floral foam. Surround the foam with assorted mosses.

Arrange 'Mariatheresia' garden roses in a narrow growing pattern. Add sweet William and *Eucalyptus* seed pods in between.

Cover the design with a bell-shaped wire dome or other decorative cloche. Stems may need to be adjusted to prevent the cover from crowding the flowers.

Insert stems of ivy through the wire frame, and allow the ivy to cascade over the edges of the pot. Tuck sheet moss and reindeer moss into the pot saucer, and add a rosebud and scattered petals to finish the presentation.

Growing

A trio of interconnected containers provides the growth point for this modern collection of anemones. Negative space between the looping grasses and the vertical flowers provides a necessary resting space between these contrasting rhythmic placements.

FRESH MATERIALS:
Eucalyptus
Curly willow
Lily grass
Anemone

Remove any foliage from the seeded *Eucalyptus,* and bend the seeded stems inside each container.

Repeat Step 1 using curly willow tips. Snake individual blades of lily grass through the *Eucalyptus*/willow stem network. Add water to each container.

Cut *Anemones* to a height at least double the height of the containers. Wedge three or four stems per container through the open spaces within the network of stems. Allow the flowers to stand roughly parallel to one another, with flowers facing naturally in varied directions.

Use additional stems of lily grass to interconnect the three containers, keeping the arching blades at a height no more than one time the height of the containers.

BRIDGES

Bridge designs feature two containers connected by flowers or other natural materials. Whether straight, arched or angled, the rhythm of a bridge design should lead the eye from one place to another, usually left to right, with at least one focal area and a secondary area of interest.

This garden-inspired bridge relies on a delicate armature of branches and grasses to support the arching blossoms. Roses, Anemones and Freesias anchor the left side while the Hydrangeas and rose on the right take on a secondary role.

FRESH MATERIALS:

Curly willow

Flexi grass

Lily grass

Veronica

Miniature calla

Rose

Carnation

Hypericum

Anemone

Hydrangea

Freesia

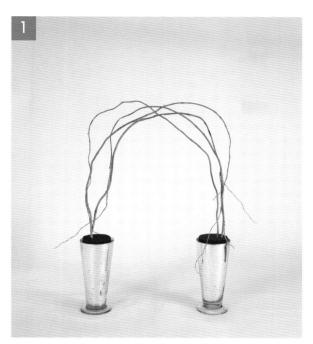

Create an arch using curly willow inserted into both containers, connecting the tip of one to the stem of another with decorative wire. Repeat with one or two additional stems to make the arch more three-dimensional.

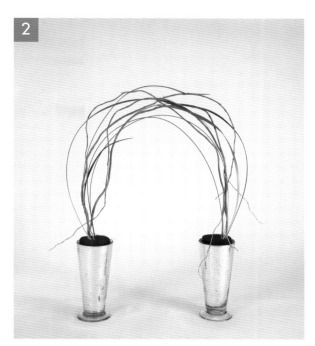

Gently bend stems of Flexi grass, and insert the ends into both containers, enhancing the willow arch. Insert lily grass into each container, threading the tips through the arch framework and wiring the tips in place, if needed.

Weave *Veronica* and miniature callas through the arch, and secure with decorative wire, if needed. If the calla stems are too straight, gently slide your thumb along one side of the stem several times until the desired curve is achieved.

Add roses, carnations and *Hypericum* at the base of each container. Add an *Anemone* to the left side and a *Hydrangea* to the right. Connect the top with the base by placing *Freesias* and *Veronica* in the intermediate level.

Bridges

This dynamic bridge utilizes a pair of matching containers in two sizes connected by a strong double diagonal of Equisetum to create eye-catching asymmetry.

FRESH MATERIALS:

Equisetum
Hypericum
Sunflower
Button mum
Solidago
Galax leaf
Honey myrtle
Italian *Ruscus*
Bupleurum
Black lichen

1 Prepare containers with floral foam. Fully insert an 18-gauge floral wire into the stem end of two *Equisetums*. Make a sharp bend in each stem about 4 or 5 inches from the end. Insert the stems into the back center of the taller container, and use wire to pin the tips to the front edge of the shorter container. Glue a single *Hypericum* berry to the tip of each *Equisetum* stem.

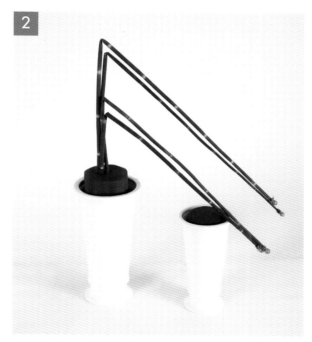

2 Repeat Step 1 with two additional *Equisetum* stems, allowing this pair to extend about 2 inches higher than the first. Adjust the stems until they are parallel with each other and the pair below. Glue a single *Hypericum* berry to each tip.

3 Create a focal point in the larger container with a single sunflower and a group of button mums tightly concentrated at the base.

4 Repeat the basing of button mums in the smaller container. Add an accent of *Solidago* behind the sunflower and finish the base of each container with *Galax*, honey myrtle, Italian *Ruscus*, *Bupleurum* and black lichen.

Bridges

A horizontal bridge provides the connection between two vases of the same style, allowing the triadic colors of orange, violet and green to provide lively harmony. Umbrella fern creates a pair of overlapping canopies that further unify the composition.

FRESH MATERIALS:

Lilium 'Heraklion'
Rosa 'Circus'
Lisianthus
Pincushion protea
Matsumoto aster
Israeli *Ruscus*
Italian miniature *Pittosporum*
Seeded *Eucalyptus*
Foxtail fern
Umbrella fern

Prepare vases with floral foam, then lay two knobby branches across the containers, and pin in place with floral wire.

Pair lilies and roses in one container and lisianthuses and pincushion proteas in the other to create independent focal areas that contrast with the colors of the containers.

Surround the focal flowers with filler elements including Matsumoto asters, Israeli *Ruscus*, Italian miniature *Pittosporum* and seeded *Eucalyptus*. Add a stem of foxtail fern extending from one container toward the other along the horizontal line of branches.

Add three or four stems of umbrella fern to each vase, keeping the stems in a tight group to form a canopy several inches above each focal area.

FRAMEWORKS

Decorative supports, such as grids and armatures, provide a great way to construct modern arrangements without floral foam. Decorative wire, marbles, branches and the like pair well with fresh flowers to provide the structural framework necessary to support creative compositions. The examples illustrated here offer options for creating frameworks in vases both tall and short, narrow and broad.

FRESH MATERIALS:

Hydrangea
Rosa 'Miranda'
Lilac
Allium
Sweet William
Rose
Spray rose
Hydrangea

This wide-mouthed vase would be challenging to design without an armature to support the flower placements. The pairing of natural and artificial stems creates an exterior frame that embraces the flowers within while providing appealing texture and interest.

Cut random branches or flower stems about twice the height of the vase. A mix of different stem colors, thicknesses and textures will make the framework more interesting. Arrange the stems in a funnel shape around the interior.

Thicken the framework with artificial branches, allowing wispy tips to extend beyond the blunt flower stem ends.

Add the largest flowers (*Hydrangeas*, garden roses, lilacs and *Alliums*) at heights similar to the branches.

Fill the remaining spaces with smaller flowers including sweet William, roses and spray roses, forming an even dome-shaped top.

Frameworks

Decorative flat wire turns a clear glass vase into a playfully striped container while providing a supportive grid over the broad opening. The resulting centerpiece is mechanically sound while appearing casually mixed.

FRESH MATERIALS:
Stock
Rosa 'Milva'
Gerbera
Parrot tulip
Craspedia
Bupleurum
Galax
Israeli *Ruscus*

1

Wrap gold and brown flat wire around the exterior of a low, rectangular vase. Starting with one color, wrap three or four times, then switch to the other color, folding the end of the wire over the edge of the vase to start and finish each wrap. Add texture by tying on raffia and wrapping it similarly among the wire.

2

Insert four or five stems of stock through the wire grid in a zigzag pattern across the top of the container.

3

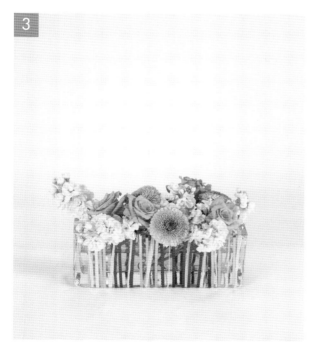

Add roses and *Gerbera*s in a scattered low profile.

4

Extend the design up and out using parrot tulips followed by *Craspedia* and *Bupleurum*. Add *Galax* and *Ruscus* to soften the container edges and provide contrast.

Frameworks

A decorative wire collar creates a framework to support this tall composition of Liatris and willow. The base elements are placed in a concentrated dome, exposing the looped wire armature accent.

FRESH MATERIALS:
Liatris
Delphinium
Curly willow
Miniature Hydrangea
Rosa 'Cool Water'
Allium
Eryngium

1

Wrap aluminum wire around a cardboard tube several times, and slide it off the tube. Flatten the wire coil, and wrap it into a disk shape. Add decorative marbles to a cylinder vase, and top with the wire armature.

2

Cut seven or eight *Liatrises* to a height nearly twice that of the vase. Insert the *Liatrises* through the central area of the armature in a radiating pattern.

3

Add shorter *Delphiniums* within the center of the *Liatris* grouping. Add tall curly willow to frame each side.

4

Place miniature *Hydrangeas* at the base of the group so they sit atop the armature. Add roses to create a focal point between the *Hydrangeas* and *Delphiniums*, then add *Alliums* and *Eryngium* to the sides.

CUTTINGS

Arrangements described here as "cuttings" have a notable loose and gardeny feeling with many random elements, often appearing freshly snipped from the garden. Abundant blooms, some with nodding heads or carefree curves, create casual compositions that break cheerfully from traditional design shapes. Combine common commercial flowers with unique garden varieties to give these designs a timeless quality.

A collection of flowering branches, garden perennials and florist favorites comfortably collide in an antique container. Flowers appear to fall naturally into place in this plum-infused composition featuring multiple areas of interest rather than a singular focal point.

FRESH MATERIALS:

Hydrangea

Lilac

Allium

Eryngium

Veronica

Trachelium

Sempervivum

Heuchera

Lamb's ear

Anemone

Lisianthus

1

Place a pair of *Hydrangeas* near the center of the container, one angled to the front, the other angled to the back. Position two stems or clusters of lilacs on angles toward each end of the container, perpendicular to the *Hydrangeas*.

2

Enhance the ends of the design with *Alliums*, *Eryngium* and *Veronica*. Connect the center placements with deep insertions of *Trachelium*.

3

Add the accent foliages at the container edges, starting with a single *Sempervivum*, followed by *Heuchera* and lamb's ear.

4

Add *Anemones* and lisianthuses for pops of color through the center and at the top.

Cuttings

Like a Dutch Master painting, this mass of graceful garden blossoms defies traditional design rules, allowing flowers to freely face downward and backward and large flowers to hover over small ones.

FRESH MATERIALS:

Amaryllis

Hydrangea

Peony

Gerbera

Dahlia

Rosa 'Peach Avalanche'

Parrot tulip

Hosta

Ninebark

Anemone

Place amaryllises in three positions above the lip of the container.

Add the *Hydrangeas* and peony beneath the amaryllises, forming a loosely mounded shape.

Extend the outline with the addition of *Gerberas*, *Dahlias*, roses and parrot tulips. Provide contrast with a few carefully placed *Hosta* leaves.

Add branches of ninebark to provide height and contrast. Finish with *Anemones* to carry the eye from tip to base.

A narrow-necked vessel provides the perfect point of radiation for a garden mix of "this and that." Single stems of some flowers, two stems of others, plus a lily that connects the tall line flowers with the base of mass flowers, create a versatile vase of garden cuttings.

FRESH MATERIALS:

Hydrangea

Delphinium

Spiraea

Lilium 'Sorbonne'

Bells-of-Ireland

Peony

Lily grass

Place two blue and two green *Hydrangeas* side by side near the lip of the vase.

Add line flowers (*Delphiniums*, bells-of-Ireland, *Spiraea*), some singly, others paired, so they extend as much as 2½ times the height of the vase.

Add a peony at the base of the line flowers just above the *Hydrangeas*. Add a single lily a half step above and to the right of the peony. Allow enough stem length for the lily to extend slightly forward, adding depth and dimension.

Group strands of lily grass into pairs and trios, and insert the groups at the edge of the container. Manipulate the strands so they flow freely into the open spaces at the base of the design.

COLLECTIONS

A gathering of vessels of like color, style or purpose becomes a floral collection with the addition of natural elements or thematic accessories. For the composition to be successful, a harmonious variety of flower types should be balanced by the repetition of at least one or two elements, whether color, texture, line or form.

Weathered terra-cotta pots and a distressed wooden tray provide the foundation for this collection of "potted" flowers. Tipped and angled pots and saucers enhance the natural look.

FRESH MATERIALS:

Cryptanthus
Rosa 'Baronesse'
Cymbidium orchid
Statice
Protea 'Susanae'
Sweet William
Garden rose
Hypericum
Dianthus 'Green Trick'
Flexi grass

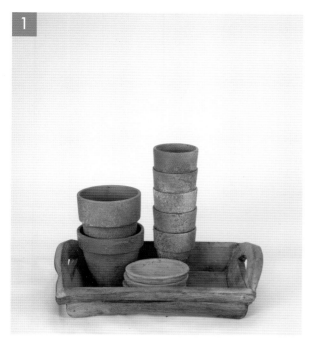

Paint a collection of terra-cotta pots and saucers with alternating bursts of dark green, medium green and white paints, and smudge the wet paint with a damp sponge to achieve an aged finish.

Plant one pot with a *Cryptanthus* or similar specimen plant. Add a plastic or foil liner and floral foam to each remaining pot, and arrange them casually in a wooden tray, positioning the largest pots near the center.

Add flowers in groups to individual pots, starting with the largest containers. Use garden roses in one and an upright *Cymbidium* orchid spray in the other, based with a cluster of statice.

Fill the remaining pots, including a single *Protea* in one, a pillow of sweet William in another, and a group of garden roses and *Hypericum* in the third. Tuck in *Dianthus* 'Green Trick' to form "mossy" tufts around the pots, and add snippets of Flexi grass to enhance the natural effect.

Collections

A shadowbox provides the perfect divided holder for a collection of vintage bottles and bowls. Muted colors and a seashell theme connect the individual containers to create a unified whole.

FRESH MATERIALS:

Peony

Parrot tulip

Ranunculus

Anemone

Hydrangea

Miniature calla

Rosa 'Mariatheresia'

Hypericum

Heather

Heuchera

1

Arrange several clear bottles and vases to create a rhythmic series across a shadowbox tray.

2

Add pink vintage bottles and bowls to fill most of the openings. Add properly prepared flower-food solution to each vessel.

3

Add one to three flowers to each container, starting with the largest flowers in the tallest vases and progressing to smaller flowers and shorter vases. Avoid massing too many flowers into one vase.

4

Add focal flowers to bowls (*Anemone* and garden rose) and add fillers (*Hypericum*, heather, *Heuchera*) among the vases as needed for texture and physical support. Finish with assorted shells and capiz disks throughout the remaining vacant openings in the tray.

Collections

*Common drinking glasses arranged like soldiers form
a strong base for a pair of angular Anthuriums.
Rolled foliage provides stability and unites the modern,
monochromatic collection.*

FRESH MATERIALS:

Aspidistra

Philodendron

Fatsia

Hypericum

Anthurium

Hydrangea

Italian variegated *Pittosporum*

Spray rose

Dianthus 'Green Trick'

Cut the stems off three *Aspidistra* leaves, two *Philodendron* leaves and a *Fatsia* leaf. Roll each *Aspidistra* leaf into a horizontal tube, with the outside of the leaf facing outward. Place each rolled leaf inside a drinking glass. Staple, if needed, to maintain the rolled form. Roll the *Fatsia* leaf, and place it inside a glass. Roll the pair of *Philodendron* leaves so they fit inside a drinking glass.

Use decorative spool wire to band three stems of tall river cane into a single unit about four times the height of the glasses. Insert the river cane bundle into the second glass. Stuff the glass with sheet moss for support, then add a cluster of *Hypericum* near the edge.

Insert a single *Anthurium* into the first and fifth glasses. Bend each *Anthurium* toward the river cane, and bind to the vertical bundle with decorative spool wire.

Accent the first glass with a single miniature *Hydrangea* and a touch of Italian variegated *Pittosporum,* and accent the fourth glass with a cluster of spray roses. Finish with *Dianthus* 'Green Trick' in the third and fifth glasses.

MODERN GROUPING

The technique of isolating flowers by type within a flower arrangement is made more modern by creating bold masses of each material and by limiting the number of groups. Line is secondary to the mass but is essential to providing rhythmic connections of the groupings. The resulting designs are striking, strong and quick to assemble.

FRESH MATERIALS:

Double-flowering tulip

Miniature calla

Freesia

Flexi grass

Hosta

Bundles of botanicals are arranged into a vase as individual units, in the same manner as single flowers would be.

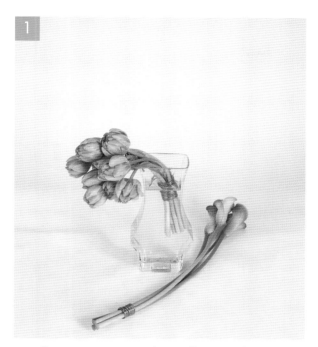

Bundle seven to nine tulips, allowing the stems to arch naturally, and band them near the base with decorative aluminum wire wrapped 10 to 12 times. Repeat this process with a group of three to five miniature callas. Position the tulips over the left edge of the vase and the callas to the right.

Remove the leaves and buds from a bunch of *Freesias*, and band the bundle near the end of the stems with decorative aluminum wire. Position the *Freesia* bundle midway between the tulips and callas.

Bind approximately one dozen stems of Flexi grass near each end with decorative aluminum wire. Position this unit to create a diagonal line to the left, forming a 'V' shape together with the calla bundle.

Create a second bundle of Flexi grass by banding near the end of the stems and just past center with decorative aluminum wire. Insert the ends of the bundle into the vase on each side of the *Freesias*, forming a loop over the blooms. Add a pair of *Hosta* leaves following the diagonal line of the Flexi grass.

Modern Grouping

A strong vertical line is formed by concentrated groupings in four quadrants of an upright, square-mouthed vase. A simple tape grid provides the mechanical support needed to keep the groups isolated and the lines parallel.

FRESH MATERIALS:

Amaryllis

Equisetum

Carnation

Hydrangea

Crisscross two pieces of clear waterproof tape across the top of the vase to create a grid with four quadrants. (White tape is used in the photo for better visibility.) Position three or four stems of amaryllises vertically with blooms clustered at the same height in the back left quadrant of the vase.

Cut 12 to15 stems of *Equisetum* to a uniform height that is approximately 3 inches taller than the amaryllises. Insert the *Equisetum* all at once into the back right quadrant of the vase.

Remove all foliage from eight to10 standard carnations, bundle them and trim the stems to a length slightly taller than the container height. Insert the carnation bundle into the front right quadrant of the vase.

Insert two or three *Hydrangeas*, one at a time, into the front left quadrant of the vase, positioning each one so the stem is straight inside the container and the flower head unifies the carnations and amaryllises.

Striped foliages pair with bold flower masses in this "masculine meets feminine" design of bold Anthuriums *and frilly peonies. Submerged* Aspidistra *leaves provide quick coverage of the mechanics, and an unexpected touch of* Leucadendron *serves as a contrasting unifier of the divergent design components.*

FRESH MATERIALS:

Aspidistra

Peony

Anthurium

Leucadendron

Position six or seven variegated *Aspidistra* leaves inside a wide-mouthed vase with the tips down and the front of each leaf facing outward. Add a block of floral foam to fit the interior of the vase, then fold the base of each *Aspidistra* leaf over so the stem, cut to about 2 inches, is inserted between the leaf and the foam block.

Add a group of five peonies to the left side of the foam, facing forward. Use two varieties of peonies for added interest.

Add a group of *Anthuriums* to the right side of the foam, their bases merging with the peonies and with each spadix angled to the right.

Add variegated *Aspidistra* leaves in a diagonal group to the left, creating a broad "V" together with the *Anthuriums*. Add a cluster of *Leucadendrons* in the gap between the *Aspidistra* leaves and *Anthuriums*.

LEAFWORK

Using foliage as a featured element gives designs of many kinds a modern look. Whether wrapped, strapped, curled or columned, leaf work can be used to create a subtle accent or strong statement. Choose foliages with inherent interest, whether shape, pattern or color, to achieve maximum impact.

Gerberas are the featured flower in this wreath-based design, but the foliages steal the show via the grasslike strapping that covers the wreath, the manipulated Aspidistra leaves and the curvaceous lily grass that radiates from the arrangement.

FRESH MATERIALS:

Lily grass
Aspidistra
Rosa 'Baronesse'
Rosa 'Mariatheresia'
Gerbera
Craspedia

1

Wrap a plastic-foam wreath with grass-patterned ribbon. Add several blades of lily grass wrapped intermittently over the ribbon. Pin the ribbon and grass in place on the underside.

2

Place a plastic tray in the center of the wreath, secure an anchor pin in the center and add a block of floral foam.

3

Insert a variegated *Aspidistra* leaf on each side of the foam block and loop it, pinning the tip to the foam. Create a base of close-set garden roses and *Gerberas* of varied colors.

4

Add a pair of tall *Gerberas* angled off center above the wreath. Tuck *Craspedia* into the base to form three clustered groups. Add lily grass radiating from the base of the tall *Gerbera* in a natural, arching manner.

Leafwork

This classic gathering of garden gems has a meadowlike quality enhanced by the modern patchwork leaf motif. Using a variety of fresh leaves, including trees, shrubs and perennials, provides greatest impact, but the foliage from the stems of a single flower type works as well.

FRESH MATERIALS:

Maple

Heuchera

Rosa 'Circus'

Ranunculus

Sunflower

Gerbera

Yarrow

Solidago

Astilbe

Kangaroo paw

Ninebark

Remove the stems from maple and *Heuchera* leaves. Apply spray adhesive to one side of each leaf. Spray from a distance of about 2 feet to prevent over-saturation and discoloration. Cover the container with overlapping layers of leaves. Facing some leaves forward and others backward in an irregular pattern provides added interest.

Add floral foam to the container, and arrange roses, *Ranunculi*, sunflowers and *Gerberas* in a radiating manner. Remove the petals from one sunflower for a showy center accent.

Enhance the edges and outline with filler flowers including yarrow, *Solidago*, *Astilbe*, kangaroo paws and ninebark.

Cut the wire edge off a piece of burlap ribbon, and fray the edges. Tie the ribbon around the neck of the container into a simple side knot.

Leafwork

A column of sword fern provides clear boundaries for the flower contents of this polychromatic composition. Wisps of bear grass, loosely sheltering the top like stray strands of hair, provide an essential relief to the otherwise concentrated and controlled collection of flowers.

FRESH MATERIALS:

Sword fern

Hydrangea

Garden rose

Sweet William

Aster

Cottage yarrow

Freesia

Ranunculus

Nigella

Bear grass

Fill a low round dish with floral foam, leaving a slight gap between the foam and the edge of the container. Cut the stems from one or two bunches of sword fern. Position individual fern fronds upright and facing outward in the gap between the foam and container. Encircle the entire container with stems of similar height.

Starting with the *Hydrangeas*, place the larger round and full flowers first, all at about the same height slightly above the fern.

Add the more delicate flowers, layering them over the larger flowers to create a somewhat flattened profile from edge to edge.

Insert the stem end of a blade of bear grass into one side of the column. Pull the blade across the top and insert the tip on the other side. Repeat with several strands of bear grass, allowing the last few tips to spring freely inward.

SPECIMENS

Monobotanical arrangements have a certain simple charm. This set of specimen designs demonstrates unconventional ways to present a single type of feature flower within modern compositions of unique containers, fillers and design techniques.

FRESH MATERIALS:
Tree fern
Bupleurum
Seeded *Eucalyptus*
Ninebark
Scabiosa

A laboratorylike vessel presents Scabiosa specimens in a garden-fresh manner. The series of four test tubes inspires the use of repetition to achieve a unified composition.

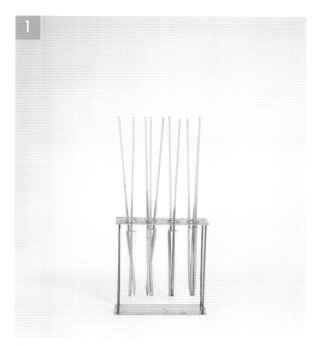

Place two or three colorful hyacinth stakes in each test tube. Fill tubes with properly prepared flower-food solution.

Add one to three stems of tree fern to each test tube at a similar height to create a continuous elevated mass of fluff.

Add *Bupleurum*, seeded *Eucalyptus* and ninebark to build layers of texture to the mass.

Add one or two stems of *Scabiosa* to each test tube, allowing the blossoms to dance freely above the mass of filler.

Specimens

A pair of Dutch Irises *hold their own in this simple but chic arrangement that uses fresh flower stems to form a geometric foundation from which the flowers emerge.*

FRESH MATERIALS:

Liatris stems

Hypericum stems

Iris

Lily grass

Sweet William

Fill the container with floral foam to a depth about 2 inches below the edge. Cut *Liatris* and *Hypericum* stems into 4-inch segments and insert into the foam along the sides of the container.

Continue adding rows of stems, leaving a 1½-inch circular opening in the center.

Add the *Irises*, one at a time, so they radiate from the center as if they are growing, making sure the stems are close enough together to appear as one plant.

Add two blades of lily grass flowing in the same direction, then add a low, tight cluster of sweet William inside the center hole.

Specimens

Layered leaves and a gravel-filled tray provide the foundation for this whimsical presentation of Alliums. Here, only capped vials are needed to provide a water source. The result is a light and free-spirited composition.

FRESH MATERIALS:

Salal

Bear grass

Allium

Place a shallow layer of gravel in the bottom of a long, low glass dish. Insert two thin stems of river cane about one inch apart into a piece of floral foam. Use a hole punch to make two holes about an inch apart in stemless salal leaves and square sections of burlap ribbon. Thread the leaves and ribbon sections intermittently onto the river cane.

Remove the river cane unit from the foam holder, and lay it across the glass dish, adjusting the leaves and ribbon sections to fit within. Add six capped water vials in between the two stems of river cane and among the salal leaves. Add several blades of bear grass to each vial.

Add three short-stemmed *Alliums* among the vials so they rest near the edge of the container.

Add three additional *Alliums* with stems several inches longer than the first to the other three vials, creating a dynamic rhythm.

WIRED

Decorative wire provides a plethora of ways to give new life to traditional flower arrangements. Spirals, coils and curls; leaf shapes and flowers; bands, braids and basket weavings can all be formed from spool wire, flat wire, aluminum wire and other such decorative elements. The trio of designs in this section showcases creative design innovations that can be achieved with your favorite decorative wire and a good pair of needle-nose pliers.

FRESH MATERIALS:

Rose

Dianthus 'Green Trick'

Lilac

Eryngium

Salal

Honey myrtle

Wire "foliage" expands the size and impact of this rosy mass. Use the leaves as a simple accent near the focal area or disperse them like a filler, as is done here, to emphasize the pleasing contrast between the natural and manmade components.

1

Fill a woodland container with floral foam, and encircle the edge with roses and *Dianthus* 'Green Trick' so the flower heads are close to the foam.

2

Add two or three colors of roses through the center, then accent with lilacs.

3

Create five or six flat wire leaf picks by shaping and coiling the wire with needle-nose pliers. Insert the wire leaves throughout the perimeter of the design.

4

Add *Eryngium*, salal and honey myrtle at the tips and edges to provide texture and contrast.

Wired

Wire coils support water vials to form a radiating centerpiece perfect for parties. Substitute any lightweight flower to achieve the color and style desired.

FRESH MATERIALS:

Gloriosa

Salal

1

Fill the container with plastic foam about ½-inch below the rim, and top with fine gravel.

2

Tightly wrap clear water vials, about 10 wraps per vial, with aluminum wire. Leave 8 to 12 inches of wire "stem" at the end. Insert the wired vials through the gravel into the plastic foam so they radiate from the center outward. Fill the vials with flower-food solution.

3

Add a single *Gloriosa* to each vial. Add salal tips, with one or two leaves each, to about half of the vials.

4

Add salal to the base, keeping it light and airy in balance with the top.

Wired

This modern interpretation of the rose bowl uses decorative wire to encase the glass container, creating an artful object from which the roses and tulips emerge. Aluminum wire coils repeat the round shapes of the flowers and container, providing a harmonious accent.

FRESH MATERIALS:

Rosa 'Patience'

Parrot tulips

Lily grass

1

Cover a 6-inch bubble bowl with a wire bouquet collar. Shape the collar over the opening and around the glass. Weave lily grass through the wire collar to create an intricate, irregular crisscross pattern.

2

Add garden roses and parrot tulips in a mounded form.

3

Add two or three aluminum wire loops over the flowers, followed by several lily grass loops and tails.

4

Use needle-nose pliers to create three coiled aluminum wire medallions. Insert the medallions near the focal area.

TWISTED

Curved lines are the focus of this trio of arrangements, providing twisted statements with a modern flair. Smooth curves and natural twists are the keys to making each of these variations universally appealing.

FRESH MATERIALS:

Dianthus 'Green Trick'
Dendrobium orchid
Bear grass
Hypericum
Cymbidium orchid

This stylish vase is elevated from the traditional radiating mix by the bear grass twists, which add lively dynamic rhythm. Allow the twists to take on natural curves and bends, or manipulate some to achieve the desired look.

Create a grid over the top of the vase using two strips of ¼-inch clear waterproof tape in each direction. Add a pillowlike mound of *Dianthus* 'Green Trick'.

Insert eight to 10 stems of *Dendrobium* orchids through the *Dianthus* in a broadly spreading and radiating fashion.

Create about a dozen bear grass twists with *Hypericum* tips by wrapping the grass with floral wire, and disperse some randomly at the edges of the vase, others rising above the orchids.

Add three or four *Cymbidium* orchids in water tubes into the center of the design, hiding the water tubes within the pillow of *Dianthus*.

Twisted

Craft foam and wired burlap ribbon lend structure to this spiraling dish of natural leaves and lichens. Work consistently in a clockwise fashion and choose contrasting textures and colors for best effect.

FRESH MATERIALS:

Aspidistra

Gerbera

Black lichen

1

Fill the dish with floral foam about half the height of the container. Cut variegated *Aspidistra* leaves lengthwise into two pieces, removing the stem and rigid center margin. Position the leaves, cut edge to the foam, in an overlapping manner against the edge of the container. Use wired burlap ribbon to continue the spiral.

2

Cut orange craft-foam sheets into 2-inch strips, and use one or two strips to continue the spiral. Intermix *Aspidistra*, burlap ribbon and craft-foam strips as the spiral progresses toward the center. Use adhesive dots, as needed, to secure layers to one another and maintain the desired circular shape.

3

Finish the spiral with a tightly coiled center of ribbon, then tuck in black lichen in a scattered fashion between the layers.

4

Add an accent of *Gerberas* rising vertically from a point off-center. Pluck the outer petals from two of the *Gerberas* to provide variety and interest.

Twisted

A traditional horizontal centerpiece is updated
with an asymmetrical placement of flowers and a
circular rhythm provided by a twisted Oasis
Midollino Stick shelter.

FRESH MATERIALS:
Israeli *Ruscus*
Huckleberry
Spiraea
Daisy mum
Dianthus 'Green Trick'
Trachelium
Freesia
Queen Anne's lace
Nigella

1

Fit a piece of floral foam into a horizontal plant saucer, bevel the foam corners and edges, and secure with waterproof tape. Pin individual Israeli *Ruscus* leaves in an overlapping fashion to the edge of the foam. Form an asymmetrical horizontal line with huckleberry.

2

Extend the line with *Spiraea*; then add daisy mums and *Dianthus* 'Green Trick' in a zigzag line from left to right.

3

Tuck *Trachelium* close to the foam between the mums and *Dianthus*. Fill out the shape with *Freesias*, Queen Anne's lace and *Nigella*.

4

Make Midollino Stick (rattan) loops, starting each piece from the front of the arrangement, looping over the top and inserting through the foam from the back to the front. Secure the tips of the Midollino Sticks at the long end of the horizontal line using decorative wire.

TRAYS

Shallow containers, saucers and pans provide ideal vessels for low-set arrangements of concentrated flower placements. The pavé technique, a manner of lining up flowers close to the foam in neat rows, curved paths or uniform clusters, fits nicely in these tray designs. By scattering flowers and varying their depth, more natural and equally appealing variations can be achieved.

Like a box of special chocolates, this rectangular tray presents a collection of varied flowers and colors in organized rows that showcase the contrasting forms and textures. The resulting "Indian blanket" composition becomes a still-life with the artful overlay of feathers.

FRESH MATERIALS:

Carnation

Dahlia

Aster

Rosa 'Shanty'

Anemone

Craspedia

Rosa 'Cool Water'

Fill the tray snugly with floral foam cut to a height half that of the container.

Starting on one end of the tray, create the first row of violet carnations, positioning them upright, with each calyx close to the foam. Use *Dahlias* to create the second row, making sure they are placed close to the carnations so no foam shows between them. Repeat this process, creating a third row with asters and a fourth row with 'Shanty' roses.

Create four more rows, using green carnations, *Anemones*, *Craspedia* and 'Cool Water' roses.

Wrap the ends of three feathers with decorative aluminum wire. Artistically lay the feathers on top of the flowers, and pin in place, if desired, using fine-gauge wire bent into hairpins.

A potpourri of garden blossoms, perennial foliage and natural vines creates a charming collection of floral gems. By anchoring the center with larger blooms, scattering filler flowers with restraint and glazing over the top with vines, a pleasing unity results.

FRESH MATERIALS:

Rosa 'Miranda'

Dahlia

Carnation

Hydrangea

Yarrow

Ranunculus

Lilac

Aster

Anemone

Heuchera

Honeysuckle

Fill the tray edge to edge with floral foam. Position one large garden rose near the center in an upright fashion close to the foam. Surround the rose with a pair of *Dahlias* on one side and a single carnation and *Hydrangea* on the other.

Broaden the collection of focal flowers by surrounding this group with yarrow in varied hues.

Add *Ranunculi, Anemones* and lilacs, filling gaps in the tray or partially layering them over other flowers.

Insert *Heuchera* foliage among the blossoms, allowing its patterned leaves and scalloped edges to be featured. Insert honeysuckle vine into the outer edges of the foam, and casually wind it among the flowers, pinning the tips into place under the blossoms.

Trays

*A round tray featuring cool colors and live succulents
is given a circular rhythm by a quartet of callas
elegantly swept sideways.*

FRESH MATERIALS:

Sempervivum

Carnation

Hydrangea

Hypericum

Miniature calla

Fill the tray snugly with floral foam to a height half that of the container. Add wooden picks to the bases of three *Sempervivum,* and position them in a triangular trio near the center of the container.

Surround the *Sempervivum* with a low group of green carnations on one side of the triangle.

Accent with three clusters of blue *Hydrangeas* placed asymmetrically. Add one or two stems of green *Hydrangeas* on another side and a cluster of *Hypericum* on the third side.

Soften the stems of four miniature callas by running fingers along one side of each stem to achieve the desired curve. Insert the callas into the floral foam, curve them around the edge, and use a long 20-gauge wire inserted through the spathe of each flower and into the foam to hold them in position.

VERTICAL

Strong, upright lines dominate these vertically inspired arrangements. Each utilizes parallelism in place of traditional radial rhythm to achieve a modern look. Proportions are maximized with tall flowers and centers of interest atop each design.

Gerberas pile up playfully in this cheerful high-low arrangement. Bare stems, positioned to maximize the impact of their natural curves, artistically fill the central void and unify the top with the base.

FRESH MATERIALS:

Gerbera
Hypericum
Craspedia

1

Line a rectangular planter with foil,
and add floral foam from edge to edge.

2

Create two rows of *Gerberas* standing at the
same height, one row in front and one in back.
Add a third row of *Gerberas* layered on top.

3

Fill the base with a low mass of *Hypericum*,
distributing one color at a time across
the container.

4

Dot the base with *Craspedia*, using a playful
rhythm and making sure some are tucked in
deeply while others extend at the edges.

Vertical

*Soldierlike flower placements form an army of
Liatrises in this modern monobotanical design.
Snipped Flexi grass provides stylish relief
from the bold parallel vertical lines.*

FRESH MATERIALS:

Liatris

Flexi grass

Fill the container with floral foam. Position about 20 stems of *Liatrises* in a parallel fashion, with a musical lift and fall to their heights.

Add tall Flexi grass in vertical groupings between the *Liatrises*.

Cut short (3- to 6-inch) pieces of Flexi grass, and insert them in irregular bunches across the base of the design. Allow the Flexi grass stems to angle in different directions to provide contrast with the parallel lines of the *Liatrises*.

Thread three or four long pieces of Flexi grass through the *Liatris* stems on angles that crisscross each other and intersect the vertical lines.

Vertical

Larkspur provides the foundation for this garden-inspired design showcasing upright flower placements with focal emphasis at the top. The design ring base reduces the number of flowers needed to fill out the columnar silhouette.

FRESH MATERIALS:

Larkspur
Heather
Veronica
Ranunculus
Miniature calla
Freesia
Queen Anne's lace
Flexi grass
Sweet William
Heuchera

Place a 6-inch floral-foam design ring in a compote, and surround it with decorative marbles.

Position six to eight stems of larkspurs around the ring, all about the same height. Add slightly shorter stems of heather in the spaces in between the larkspurs.

Add three or four tall stems of *Veronica* followed by *Ranunculi*, miniature callas and *Freesias*, extending each near the top.

Add Queen Anne's lace to the upper level of the design, followed by a few random blades of Flexi grass. Complete the base with sweet William and *Heuchera* foliage.

PARTITIONED

This trio of arrangements showcases the modernity that can be achieved by dividing a composition into sections or compartments. Whether using a single container or several compatible vessels, color-blocking and flower-blocking provide fresh ways of organizing the floral materials into a unified whole.

This voluminous arrangement utilizes four matching flat-sided vases to segregate the flower types and ease assembly. Using tall linear flowers in some vases and shorter mass and focal flowers in others provides variety and assures interest from tip to base.

FRESH MATERIALS:

Delphinium

Larkspur

Hydrangea

Dendrobium orchid

Stock

Veronica

Peony

Fill the first vase with a massed column of *Delphiniums* and larkspurs. Add a *Hydrangea* on the left side at the lip of the vase.

Fill the second vase with *Dendrobium* orchids, positioning them freely, with some upright and others arching forward. Place the second vase side by side with the first.

Fill the third vase with a bunch of stock, then add a few *Veronica*. Place the third vase side by side with the second.

Fill the fourth vase with a low mass of peonies, and position it side by side with the third vase. Adjust the flowers, as needed, to fill any gaps between the four vases.

Partitioned

In this garden-inspired arrangement, plants and flowers combine to create a multi-tiered composition with sunflowers forming a natural stem lattice. The resulting partitions house horizontal rows of contrasting blues and golds accented with pops of orange to unify with the container.

FRESH MATERIALS:

Sunflower

Sansevieria

Iris

Matsumoto aster

Alstroemeria

Gerbera

Trachelium

Hyacinth

Ranunculus

Lily grass

Curly willow

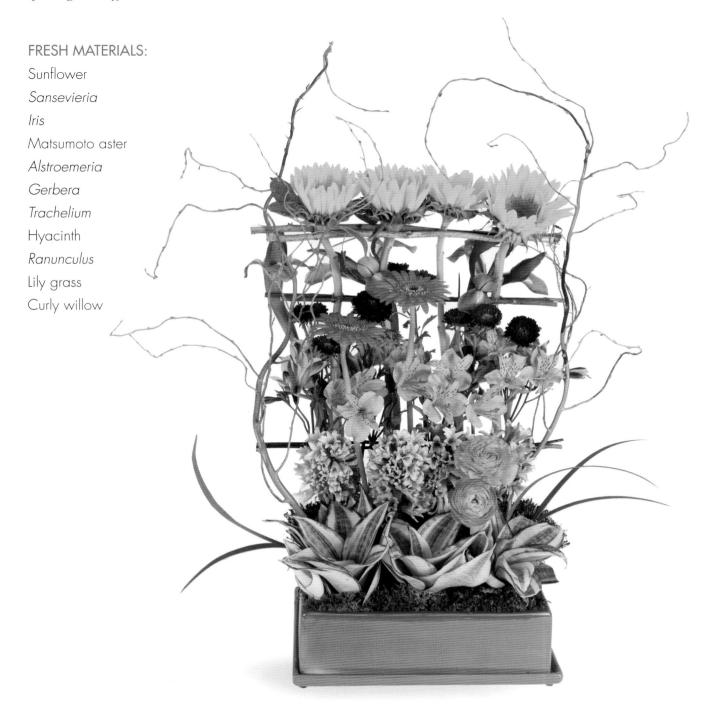

1

Line a low planter with foil, and fill it edge to edge with floral foam. Align four tall sunflowers in the back of the foam, all at the same height. Using bind wire, attach stems or sticks beneath the heads of the sunflowers, at two levels, to create a lattice. Position three *Sansevieria* plants in a row at the front edge of the container.

2

Create a row of *Irises* behind the lattice at a level just below the sunflowers. Add a row of Matsumoto asters followed by a row of *Alstroemerias*. Then, add a pair of stair-stepped *Gerberas* in a high position off-center to the left.

3

Place a row of *Trachelium* close to the foam behind the *Sansevierias*. Add a row of hyacinths in the gap between the *Sansevierias* and *Alstroemerias*. Then, add a pair of stair-stepped *Ranunculi* in a low position off-center to the right.

4

Add a few blades of lily grass arching outward from the sides of the design. Frame the arrangement using curly willow on each side, with the curves of the branches angled inward.

Partitioned

Trays, cubes and bud vases combine to form a shadowbox-like composition featuring partitions filled with unique floral components. Repetition of colors and flower types within the boxes creates unity while the textures and forms of marbles and mosses add interest.

FRESH MATERIALS:
Dianthus 'Green Trick'
Rosa 'Sanaa'
Rosa 'Sweetness'
Carnation
Black lichen
Reindeer moss

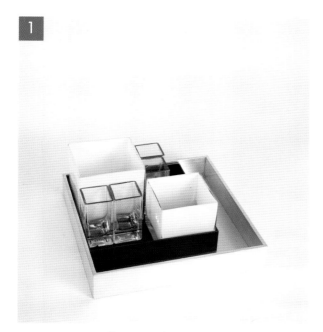

Organize a collection of trays, cubes and square bud vases into a large tray to create a partitioned "container." Fill the cubes with floral foam.

Fill the lowest partitions with green marbles, black lichen, reindeer moss and *Dianthus* 'Green Trick'.

Fill each cube with nine matching roses, forming three rows of three flowers. Tuck in sheet moss, as needed, to cover visible floral foam.

Add a single short-stemmed carnation to each bud vase, creating patterned placements.

SPHERES

The round form is a classic in floral design, yet it offers limitless potential for variation and modernization. Here, fresh approaches are offered for a traditional globular composition, a wedged variation and a bubble bowl with a contemporary twist. Though mechanically quite different from one another, each results in a comfortably familiar and equally appealing spherical design.

Fresh redbud leaves provide a natural skin for this globular composition of garden blossoms. Slicing a wedge out of the floral-foam sphere allows the flowers to nestle comfortably into the spherical base.

FRESH MATERIALS:

Redbud leaves

Lilac

Seeded *Eucalyptus*

Hypericum

Bupleurum

Spray rose

Ranunculus

Anemone

Miniature calla

1

Slice a wedge out of a floral-foam sphere, making sure not to slice deeper than the center. Soak the sphere by free-floating in properly prepared flower-food solution.

2

Apply spray adhesive to the backs of several stemless redbud leaves. Cover the sphere with leaves, overlapping the base of each leaf with the tip of the next and folding leaves over the edges into the wedge.

3

Fill the crevice deeply with lilacs. Layer seeded *Eucalyptus* over the lilacs in a forward flowing line.

4

Insert *Hypericum*, *Bupleurum*, spray roses and additional redbud leaves to add volume. Then, nestle *Ranunculi*, *Anemones* and miniature callas into the bed of fillers to top out the design.

Spheres

A mix of garden and hybrid tea roses creates volume in this deconstructed topiary design. The perfect spherical form offers a bold contrast to the organic driftwood base.

FRESH MATERIALS:

Rosa 'Baronesse'

Rosa 'Mariatheresia'

Rosa 'Hypnose'

Sweet William

Spiraea

Bupleurum

Cut the stems of the garden roses to about 1¾ inches in length, and distribute them evenly throughout the sphere, inserting them so the base of each flower is in contact with the floral foam.

Add the hybrid tea roses in between the garden roses, allowing slight variations in depth.

Add sweet William, followed by *Spiraea* and *Bupleurum,* to fill the remaining spaces between the flowers.

Cradle the finished sphere into the crook of a strong piece of driftwood.

Spheres

Callas and carnation petals pair pleasingly in this bubble bowl duo that utilizes decorative flat wire to unify the parts. Simple mechanics and a stem-to-spathe trick make this design quick and easy to assemble.

FRESH MATERIALS:

Miniature calla

Carnation

Place a looped piece of flat wire inside a large bubble bowl, and spread out the wire to fill the space. Soften the stems of six or seven miniature callas by sliding a thumb along one side of each stem while applying gentle pressure. Position the stems in the bubble bowl to create a circular motion.

2

Arrange the miniature callas evenly throughout the bowl, placing the stem of one calla into the spathe of another so stem ends are hidden. Add a second layer of looped flat wire above the miniature callas.

3

Fill a 6-inch bubble bowl with carnation petals, and place the bowl in the center of the larger bubble bowl.

4

Wrap a length of flat wire into a spiral about the size of the small bubble bowl. Place the tight center of the wire spiral inside the small bubble bowl, and allow the remainder of the spiral to wrap around the interior of the large bubble bowl.

CLOUDS

Focal flowers take a back seat to cloudlike puffs of fillers in this modern collection of mass designs, where texture is the primary featured element. Simple flower formulas keep the focus on shape and style, making these easy to modify with many different flower and foliage combinations.

A containerized version of the classic cloud bouquet, this design uses baby's breath (Gypsophila) to encase a loosely structured round mound. Adjust the density of the filler to achieve a lighter cloud or to blur the flower edges and blend the colors.

FRESH MATERIALS:
Rosa 'Peach Avalanche'
Godetia
Stock
Gerbera
Gypsophila 'Million Stars'
Hypericum
Black lichen

Fill the container with floral foam, and cover loosely with black lichen. Add roses and *Godetia* to form a loose, low mound.

Extend the shape with stocks and *Gerberas*, allowing comfortable negative space between the placements.

Add the baby's breath in layers, starting with short stems inserted deeply, followed by tall, billowy stems that extend beyond the flowers.

Add *Hypericum*, as needed, to fill the gaps and unify the flower base with the filler overlay.

Clouds

*Tree fern and Solidago combine to form a treelike canopy
over this dense composition of mosses and blossoms.
The puffy cloud of filler is underscored by vibrant Freesias
forming a dividing line between the tightly constructed
base and the loosely constructed top.*

FRESH MATERIALS:

Solidago
Tree fern
Freesia
Bells-of-Ireland
Carnation
Reindeer moss
Black lichen

1

Fill the container with floral foam, and cover lightly with sheet moss. Strip the foliage from eight to 10 stems of *Solidago*, and position them side by side in a loose row several inches above the container. Add stems of tree fern in between to create a spreading mass.

2

Use one bunch of *Freesias* to create a line of color just beneath the fillers.

3

Cut one or two stems of bells-of-Ireland into segments just above each whorl of inflated "bells." Insert the segments rhythmically across the container so the "bells" rest against the mossy base. Add three carnations similarly positioned close to the foam.

4

Use reindeer moss, black lichen, bark chips and/or mulch to enhance the base with earthy elements.

Clouds

Garden roses peek from beneath a billowy cloud of Queen Anne's lace while Bupleurum and lily grass provide a natural understory to this modern composition. Eight diminutive bottle vases, when grouped into a larger mass, provide a harmonic foundation that simplifies the design process.

FRESH MATERIALS:

Bupleurum

Queen Anne's lace

Rosa 'Patience'

Lily grass

Group eight square bottle vases into two rows of four. Fill the vases with *Bupleurum* to create a unified mass.

Add Queen Anne's lace to each vase at a height twice that of the *Bupleurum* until a loosely unified mass is achieved.

Add one or two garden roses per vase, tucking them in at the juncture between the *Bupleurum* and Queen Anne's lace and varying the depth from front to back.

Add about three stems of lily grass to each vase, positioning the grass to flow gracefully at the edges.

CONTAINED

Flowers contained within boundaries provide a sense of comfort and charm. Whether walled by the container, caged within a shelter or embraced in the crook of a branch, flowers that are contained create curiosity and intrigue. The designs within this set are contained in uniquely different ways, yet they share a common concentration of low, dense flowers providing much for the viewer to explore.

Daisy mums, Hydrangeas and whimsical Veronica find shelter beneath a canopy of grasses and barked wire. Wooden eggs provide a welcome contrast to the flowers and foliage, and an upright foliage collar offers a refreshing organic border.

FRESH MATERIALS:

Salal

Hydrangea

Honey myrtle

Italian variegated *Pittosporum*

Daisy mum

Veronica

Flexi grass

Bear grass

1

Fill the container with floral foam, leaving a slight gap at the edges. Remove the stems from fresh salal leaves, and slide the base of each leaf between the container and foam to create a border. Face the fronts of the leaves outward.

2

Create a low dense base with two or three *Hydrangeas* surrounded by sprigs of honey myrtle and Italian variegated *Pittosporum*.

3

Add eight to 10 daisy mums "growing" randomly at a level slightly above the greens. Place three wooden eggs in staggered positions within the base.

4

Add three to five *Veronica*, allowing the tips to curve naturally toward the edges of the container. Use Flexi grass, bear grass and barked wire to create a crisscrossed shelter over the top of the design.

Contained

A thicket of artificial branches, artistically curved inward, creates a cozy setting for this bowl of cool-colored garden blossoms anchored by a faux crystal geode. Snipped segments of Equisetum cut a clever path through the center while black lichen injects an unexpected contrast at the edge.

FRESH MATERIALS:

Galax leaf
Hydrangea
Dianthus 'Green Trick'
Carnation
Godetia
Equisetum
Anemone
Black lichen

1

Fill the bowl with floral foam; then create a collar of *Galax* leaves around the edge. Encircle the bowl with artificial branches, using longer branches along the back and sides and shorter branches in front. Bend the branches inward.

2

Nestle a faux crystal geode into the foam in an off-center position. Surround the geode with *Hydrangeas* and *Dianthus* 'Green Trick' inserted close to the foam.

3

Layer carnations and *Godetia* over the base flowers to fill gaps and provide contrast.

4

Create a pathway of *Equisetum* stems using cut segments in stair-stepped clusters. Add two or three *Anemones* to create a focal area. Tuck in small clumps of black lichen, as needed, to fill gaps and provide texture.

Contained

A lasso of barked wire provides a woven window into the basin of this Southwest-inspired bowl design. Succulents, tropicals and garden blossoms converge well below the rim, with only a wand of miniature callas escaping the confines of the container.

FRESH MATERIALS:

Miniature calla

Sunflower

Pincushion protea

Succulent

Dahlia

Yarrow

Hypericum

Button mum

Seeded *Eucalyptus*

Honey myrtle

Black lichen

Fill the lower 2 inches of a large, deep bowl with floral foam. Bind three or four miniature callas into a wand using several wraps of decorative aluminum wire, and lay them into the bowl so the flower heads extend over the edge. Add three sunflowers and three pincushion proteas overlapping each other close to the foam.

Add two or three succulent rosettes followed by *Dahlias* and yarrow in subtly stair-stepped placements.

Insert *Hypericum*, button mums, seeded *Eucalyptus*, honey myrtle and black lichen in scattered but controlled positions throughout the bowl, filling gaps and adding texture.

Loop barked wire into a loose "lasso" slightly larger than the bowl, and bind it with the free ends of the wire. Set the "lasso" on top of the bowl, pinching the wire in several places around the edge to hold it in position.

STILL LIFE

Like painted works of art, still-life arrangements feature inanimate objects often selected to convey a particular spirit or theme. Flowers may be featured but generally share the attention with gathered items such as fruits, nuts, eggs, seashells, books, coins and bottles. Each still-life example demonstrated here depicts a moment in time that takes the viewer to a familiar place and stirs emotions unique to the individual.

Seashells and tropical Anthuriums *provide the ocean inspiration for this clean and simple still-life. A coil of* Hypericum *berries lends visual rhythm and connects the color across the design.*

FRESH MATERIALS:
Miniature calla
Anthurium
Hypericum

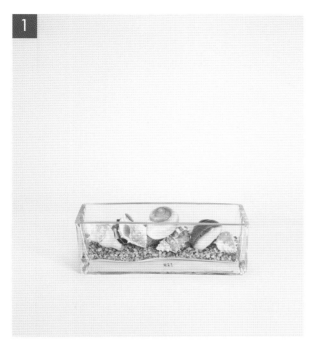

Fill the vase with a layer of pea gravel, then add a collection of seashells artistically stacked and arranged to fill most of the container.

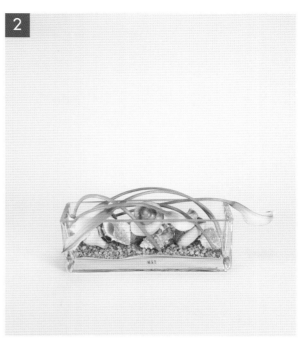

Develop a crisscrossed grid of miniature callas over the shells, with flower heads flowing in both directions, some inside and others outside the vase. Manipulate the calla stems, as needed, to develop graceful arching lines.

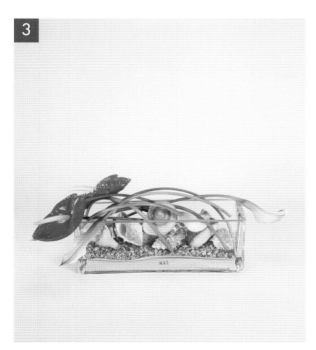

Thread four *Anthuriums* through the grid of calla stems, with all flower heads grouped to the same end of the vase. Top the *Anthuriums* with an additional miniature calla flowing in the same direction.

String *Hypericum* berries onto beading wire by piercing through the base of each berry and emerging through the tip. Loop the *Hypericum* strand through the container, then top the container with a few more shells.

Still Life

A vase of flowers creates a colorful bookend in this still-life nod to the formal home library. Coordinated bookcovers and feather-pen-inspired accessories support the shared emphasis on flowers and objects.

FRESH MATERIALS:

Rosa 'Circus'

Miniature calla

Asiatic lily

Pincushion protea

Eryngium

Solidago

Kangaroo paw

Honey myrtle

Hydrangea

Hyacinth

Yarrow

Salal

On a tray, create a faux bookshelf with a vase, shells and small books wrapped in coordinated decorative paper.

Design the flowers in a loose mass, starting with the roses, miniature callas, lilies and pincushion proteas. Use the assorted fillers to fill out the shape. Add hyacinths and *Hydrangea* accents to the right, and finish with yarrow.

Position feathers to extend the height and add a touch of whimsy.

Spray the front of two salal leaves with adhesive, and press the leaves on old book pages. Trim around the leaf edges, and add the leaves to the lip of the container.

Still Life

Needled branches and glossy foliage dominate the flowers in this woodland still-life featuring a fallen nest and scattered pine cones. Dianthus 'Green Trick' mimics moss, and artificial branches add thorny notes for added texture and realism.

FRESH MATERIALS:

Scotch pine

Pittosporum

Dianthus 'Green Trick'

Hydrangea

Lay a scotch pine branch across a wooden tray. Wire in the nest, and add eggs.

Tuck in sprigs of *Pittosporum* and *Dianthus* 'Green Trick'. Place three *Hydrangeas* into water tubes, and position them around the nest.

Add pine cones in the openings, using wire, as needed, to secure them in place.

Bend artificial branches to create curved lines, and position them so they arch over the nest to provide a shelter.

REVERSE

Taking liberties with the standard rules of proportion, the arrangements in this section reverse the size relationships typically applied in traditional floral design. A tall container houses a low composition, a broad and boxy vessel holds a slim cascading design and an upright vase features the largest flowers at the top. Controlled placements and contemporary techniques give these reverse proportions a modern edge.

This upright composition gives the vertical design style a new flair with fresh materials flowing downward instead of up. Equisetum *emphasizes the lean line of the container while tailored bear grass loops and trails with a dynamic rhythm around the vibrant floral center.*

FRESH MATERIALS:

Equisetum	Bear grass
Ranunculus	*Rosa* 'Baronesse'
Cymbidium orchid	*Allium*
Button mum	Carnation
Hypericum	*Delphinium*
Honey myrtle	Flexi grass

1

Fill the container with floral foam to a height about 1 inch above the top edge. Use short pieces of floral wire to pin 10 stems of *Equisetum* upside down to the side of the foam. Trim the *Equisetum* stem ends to an even length about 3 inches above the container. Secure the stems in place against the side of the container with mesh coil ties.

2

Place two garden roses in stair-step fashion in the center of the foam. Tuck two stair-stepped *Ranunculi* beneath the roses, then tightly mass a single *Allium*, *Cymbidium* orchid and carnation around the roses to form a low mass.

3

Add single blossoms or small clusters of button mums, *Delphiniums*, *Hypericum* and honey myrtle to fill gaps and add texture while maintaining a tightly concentrated mass.

4

Create a pair of sheltering loops over the floral center using Flexi grass and bear grass. Create a wire-wrapped unit of bear grass with a *Hypericum* berry tip, and insert it at the point where the grass loops end. Curl the tip upward toward the floral center.

119

Reverse

Bleached willow sticks form a reverse tripod foundation for this modern twist on the triangular design form. Lilies share the spotlight with Oasis Midollino Stick triangles that cage the stems and lend an artistic flair.

FRESH MATERIALS:

Lilium 'Trebiano'

Hypericum

Fill the container with floral foam level with the rim of the container. Insert three bleached willow sticks radiating from the center outward to form a triangular top.

Create six or seven triangles of varying sizes using rattan Midollino Sticks bound with decorative wire. Slide the triangles onto the bleached willow framework, pitching them at varied angles. Secure the triangles in place with decorative wire or adhesive dots.

Insert two stems of lilies into the center of the triangular frame so the largest flowers extend just above the top of the frame. Add a third stem of lilies between these two.

Use individual *Hypericum* berries inserted into the foam base to create an inner ring around the willow sticks. Repeat this process to create an outer ring around the container edge. Fill in between with additional *Hypericum* berries until all foam is covered.

Reverse

Equisetum *stems create a natural armature through which fresh flowers are inserted into a broad and blocky vase. Trimmed plumosa fern provides a light shelter over the linear focal area featuring a horizontal path of* Gerbera *blossoms and a young* Cryptanthus *plant.*

FRESH MATERIALS:

Equisetum

Gerbera

Cryptanthus

Spray rose

Hydrangea

Delphinium

Hypericum

Brunia

Italian variegated *Pittosporum*

Honey myrtle

Seeded *Eucalyptus*

Plumosa fern

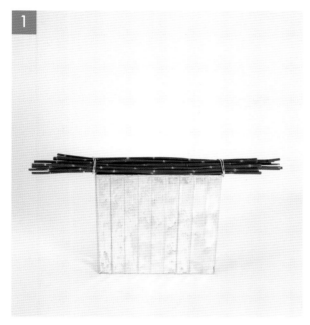

Loosely gather 10 to 12 stems of *Equisetum*, with half of the stems aligned in each direction to create a linear bundle about twice the length of the container. Center the bundle on top of the container, and bind with aluminum wire on each side.

Fill the central portion of the bundle with a zigzag line of *Gerberas* and *Cryptanthus*, inserting the *Gerbera* stems through spaces in the *Equisetum* bundle and using a wood pick to create a stem for insertion of the *Cryptanthus*.

Dot the base with spray roses, *Hydrangeas* and other small textured fillers to connect the focal materials and extend the horizontal path.

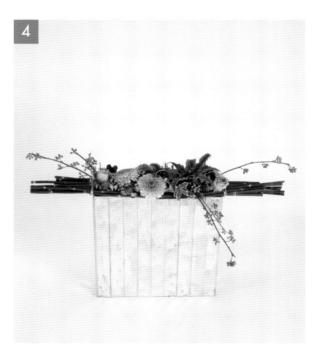

Radiate seeded *Eucalyptus* on angles away from the base of the *Gerberas* and the *Cryptanthus* to relieve the rigid horizontal line. Create a shelter over the design using long pieces of plumosa fern flowing from left to right. Trim the plumosa, as needed, to achieve a light veil.

CREDITS

AUTHOR AND FLORAL DESIGNER

Teresa P. Lanker is chair of the Horticultural Technologies Division at The Ohio State University ATI. She also is the coordinator of the Floral Design and Marketing Technology program and teaches courses in floral design, commercial floristry and related areas of horticulture. Terry has worked in the flower business since her first job, at age 16, at Amlings Flowerland in Chicago. As an educator, she enjoys sharing her love of flowers and the floral industry with new students young and old.

FLORAL DESIGNER

Talmage McLaurin, AIFD, began his floral career in a family-owned flower business. In 1990, he launched a 23-year publishing career with Florists' Review Enterprises. Talmage has made presentations at seven National Symposiums of the American Institute of Floral Designers (AIFD), and, in 2003, he co-chaired the National Symposium, "The Prairie School." In 2008, Talmage received AIFD's "Award of Distinguished Service to the Floral Industry."

FRESH FLOWERS

All the flowers used to make the arrangements in this book were provided by DVFlora with locations in Balitmore, MD; Bogota, Colombia; Cromwell, CT; Edison, NJ; Miami, FL; Oxnard, CA; Sewell, NJ; Shrewsbury, MA. www.dvflora.com 800-676-1212

florists'review

President: Frances Dudley, AAF

Author: Teresa P. Lanker

Floral Designers: Teresa P. Lanker, Talmage McLaurin, AIFD

Editors: Amy Bauer, David Coake, Shelley Urban

Graphic Designer: Linda Kunkle Park

Production Designers: Holly Cott, Nicole Robinson

Modern Flower Arranging: Step-by-Step Instructions for Modern Designs
was produced by Florists' Review Enterprises, Inc., Topeka, Kansas.
www.floristsreview.com

Photography, design and typesetting by
Florists' Review Enterprises, Inc., Topeka, Kansas

Printed in China

ISBN: 978-0-9854743-3-1

Florists' Review is the only independent trade magazine for professional
florists in the United States. In addition to serving the needs of retail
florists through its monthly publication, Florists' Review Enterprises has a
bookstore and products division that supplies books and merchandise
to all who are interested in floral design. For more information, visit
www.floristsreview.com or call 800-367-4708.

4

6

8

10

12

14

16

18

20

22

24

26

28

30

32

34

36

38

40

42

44

46

48

50

52

54

56

58

60

62

64

66

68

70

72

74

76

78

80

82

84

86

88

90

92

94

96

98

100

102

104

106

108

110

112

114

116

118

120

122

florists'review

WWW.FLORISTSREVIEW.COM

800-367-4708